Cambridge English Readers

....

Level 1

Series editor: Philip Prowse

Next Door to Love

Margaret Johnson

CAMBRIDGE
UNIVERSITY PRESS

CAMBRIDGE
UNIVERSITY PRESS

University Printing House, Cambridge CB2 8BS, United Kingdom

One Liberty Plaza, 20th Floor, New York, NY 10006, USA

477 Williamstown Road, Port Melbourne, VIC 3207, Australia

314–321, 3rd Floor, Plot 3, Splendor Forum, Jasola District Centre, New Delhi – 110025, India

79 Anson Road, #06–04/06, Singapore 079906

Cambridge University Press is part of the University of Cambridge.

It furthers the University's mission by disseminating knowledge in the pursuit of education, learning and research at the highest international levels of excellence.

www.cambridge.org
Information on this title: www.cambridge.org/9780521605625

First published 2005
Reprinted 2019

Printed in the United Kingdom by Hobbs the Printers Ltd

A catalogue record for this publication is available from the British Library

ISBN 978-0-521-60562-5 Paperback

Illustrations by Chris Pavely

Contents

People in the story

Stella: a cook in a restaurant
Tony: Stella's neighbour
Daisy: Tony's daughter
Janet: Stella's best friend
Kathy: Tony's ex-wife
Klaus: works with Stella

Chapter 1 *The man at number three*

My friend Janet looked out of my living room window. 'Who is *that*?' she asked.

I went to look. 'He lives here,' I said.

'He lives here . . . in Bridge Street?' Janet asked.

'Yes,' I said. 'At number three, next door to me. He's my new neighbour.'

Janet smiled. 'He's very tall,' she said. 'And I like his black hair.'

'Janet,' I said. 'Come away from the window.' I didn't want my new neighbour to see us.

She turned to me.

'It's OK,' she said, 'I'm just looking. I don't want a new man. I've got David.'

David is Janet's boyfriend.

'I'm only thinking of you,' she said. 'You need a new boyfriend. What's your neighbour's job?' she asked me.

'I don't know,' I said.

'Well, how old is he?'

I looked at her. 'I don't know, Janet,' I said.

'Has he got a girlfriend?'

'Janet,' I said, 'I don't know anything about him. I saw him yesterday and we said "hello". That's all.'

Janet always wanted me to go out and meet new men.

'You need to go out, Stella,' she often told me. 'You need to meet new people. New men.'

But I didn't want to meet new men, and I didn't want a boyfriend. I knew boyfriends didn't always make you happy. My last boyfriend, James, didn't make me happy.

Janet looked at me. 'You're thinking about James,' she said. Janet often knows what I'm thinking. 'Don't think about him,' she said. 'He wasn't any good for you. But you mustn't think all men are bad. Your neighbour looks nice.'

'Stop talking about him!' I told her. And we laughed.

Janet left my house at about six o'clock, and I went up to change for my tennis class. My neighbour was out in his garden. It was August and there were lots of flowers in all the gardens. The flowers in the garden at number three were yellow, red, orange and pink. Happy colours. But my neighbour didn't look happy.

'You're sad,' I thought as I looked down at him. 'Why? Why are you sad?' Then he looked up, and I came away from the window quickly.

I saw my neighbour again the next morning, in the street. He looked tired.

'Hello,' I said. 'It's a beautiful day.'

'Yes,' he said. 'It's hot again. Too hot for work.' Then he smiled at me. 'My name's Tony,' he said. 'Tony Bryant.'

I took his hand. 'Hello, Tony,' I said. 'I'm Stella. Stella Greenwood.'

'Good to meet you, Stella,' he said.

I didn't see Tony the next day, or the day after that. Then, on the Friday morning I heard him on the phone next door. The houses in Bridge Street are small and you can sometimes hear people speaking. And I heard everything that Tony Bryant said that morning. He was very angry.

'You can't do this, Kathy!' he said. 'You can't do this to me again! I want to see her. Please, Kathy. Don't do this!'

I sat at my breakfast table and listened.

'Kathy? Kathy? Oh!' I heard Tony say, and then he put the phone down.

I ate an apple and thought about Tony Bryant. Who was Kathy? And what was Tony afraid of? Because I *knew* he was afraid of something.

There's something Janet always says to me, something that's very important to her. She says, 'When you want to do something, just do it. Don't stop and think about it! Don't wait. Just do it!'

And that's what I did after I heard Tony Bryant on the phone.

I didn't stop and think. I put my apple down on the table and went to the house next door.

I had to wait a long time. Then Tony answered the door.

'Yes?' he said. He didn't look very happy. And then, of course, I didn't know what to say.

'Yes?' he said again. 'What do you want, Stella?'

I started to blush then and my face felt hot. 'I . . . I wanted . . .' I started to say. 'I just wanted to know . . .' And I stopped.

'You wanted to know . . . what?' Tony said.

'Well, are you all right?' I asked, and he looked at me. His face was cold, but I thought he was just sad or angry about something.

'Yes, thank you,' he said. 'I'm all right.'

I blushed some more. 'Oh,' I said. 'OK, good. That's good. Good. Well, bye then!' And I left quickly.

But then Tony called after me. 'Stella! Wait!'

I stopped and looked back at him.

'I'm sorry,' he said. 'It was nice of you to ask. Have you got time to come in for a coffee?'

I looked at my watch. It was nine o'clock. 'Not now,' I said. 'Sorry, Tony. I'm late for work.'

'OK,' he said. 'I'm going away today. But come for coffee next weekend.'

I smiled at him. 'Thank you,' I said.

Chapter 2 *Flowers from Daisy*

The next weekend it was hot again and I wanted to sit in the sun all day. I took a book and a drink and went out into the garden. And that's when I heard the child.

'I'm going out,' the child said, and then a small face looked at me from Tony's garden. A little girl's face.

'Hello,' the little girl said to me. She had lots of black hair under her big sun hat.

'Hello,' I said. 'Who are you?'

'Daisy,' she said. 'That's a flower. I like flowers. Do you like flowers?'

I smiled at her. She was about five or six years old. But who was she? Then Tony came out. He stood next to Daisy, and I knew who she was.

'Hello,' he said to me. 'This is my daughter, Daisy.'

'Hello Daisy,' I said, and I saw that Tony was happy. Very happy.

'Can she come to tea with us, Daddy?' Daisy asked her father.

'*She* has a name,' Tony told her. 'She's called Stella.'

'OK, can Stella come to tea with us?' Daisy asked.

Tony smiled at me. 'Of course she can,' he said.

We sat in Tony's garden and Daisy told me all about her cat. She talked a lot.

'He's black and white,' she said, 'like a cow. I call him Moo-Moo, like the noise cows make. But he drinks milk. Cows don't drink milk.'

'Cows *make* milk,' Tony told her. He smiled at me over Daisy's head.

Daisy looked at him. 'I know that, Daddy!' she said. 'I'm not a little girl anymore!' And she went to look at the flowers.

'She's lovely,' I told Tony.

He looked at his daughter and smiled. 'Yes,' he said, 'she is.' Then he looked sad. 'But I don't see her very often because her mother and I aren't together now.'

'*That's* why he's sad,' I thought. 'I'm sorry, Tony,' I said.

'I'm OK, now,' Tony said quickly.

He smiled at me. 'Anyway, how are you? How was your week?'

'It was good,' I said. 'There was a lot to do at work.'

Tony smiled. 'What do you do?'

'I'm one of the cooks at Marcello's Italian Restaurant.'

'You're a chef?' he said. 'That's a good job.'

'Yes,' I said. 'I love it. What about you? What do you do?'

'I work with computers,' Tony told me. Daisy came over to us again. 'These are for you,' she said, and she gave us some flowers.

'Thank you, Daisy,' we said. She smiled at us and then ran away across the garden.

'Leave some flowers in the garden, please, Daisy!' Tony told her. 'They look nice there.'

I put my face into the red and orange flowers. They were beautiful.

'I think she likes you,' Tony told me.

I smiled at him. 'I like her too.'

Tony looked at the flowers in his hand. 'Some of me dies when Daisy's away from me,' he said. Then he looked at me. 'Daisy lives with her mother, Kathy, and Kathy's husband, Cameron.' Tony looked away. 'Daisy's got a new family now,' he said.

Well, now I knew. Kathy, the woman on the phone, was Daisy's mother. 'That's sad,' I said.

Tony smiled, but he wasn't happy. 'Yes. Oh, I know Daisy likes Cameron. But he isn't her father. I am.'

'How often do you see Daisy?' I asked.

'Not very often. But she sees Cameron every day. Anyway, she's here today,' Tony said. 'And I'm happy.'

Daisy looked over and smiled at us. I smiled back at her. 'I can understand computers,' Tony told me. 'I know what they're going to do. But I don't always understand people.'

I thought about James and all his girlfriends. 'No, we don't always know what people are going to do,' I said.

Next day I met up with Janet in town. We went to a café for a drink. She asked about Tony, and I told her about my afternoon with him.

'Did he ask you to go out with him?' she wanted to know.

'No!' I said. 'He's just my neighbour.' But I blushed and Janet saw.

'You like him,' she told me.

'Yes, all right,' I said. 'I do like him. But he's a very sad man. I think he's still in love with Daisy's mother, Kathy.'

Janet looked at me. 'But you said Kathy is Cameron's wife now.'

'Yes,' I said. 'Kathy is Cameron's wife. But Tony still thinks about the time when they were a family . . . him, Daisy and Kathy. I don't think he understands why everything changed.'

'That is sad,' Janet said. Then she looked at me. 'Well,' she said, 'you need a man to laugh with, so I don't think Tony is good for you.'

'I don't need a man, Janet,' I told her. 'I'm happy without a boyfriend.'

But Janet looked at me. 'Everybody needs someone, Stella,' she said.

Chapter 3   *Everybody needs someone*

The next day lots of people came to Marcello's Restaurant and I had lots of food to cook. The weather was still warm, and in the kitchen it was very, very hot. I was happy to have lots to do. I didn't want to think about Janet's words. 'Everybody needs someone, Stella.'

But of course I did think about them . . . all day. I also thought about James and how he made me sad. Then I thought about Tony and how Kathy made him sad. And then Daisy . . .

'They all enjoyed their food,' Klaus, one of the waiters, told me in the afternoon.

I liked Klaus. He was over in England from Germany for six months and he was always happy.

'Good,' I replied.

'Do you want to go out with me tonight, Stella?' Klaus asked me. 'I'm going to the cinema. Can you come?'

I thought about Janet's words again. 'Everybody needs someone, Stella.' Then I looked at Klaus and smiled. 'Yes, OK,' I said.

When I got home at six o'clock, Tony was taking things out of his car. 'Hi, Stella,' he said.

I smiled at him. He looked good in his black work trousers and white shirt. 'Hi Tony. How are you?'

'Very well, thank you,' he replied. 'It's good to see you.'

'Yes,' I said. 'It's good to see you too.'

'I'm going out for a drink tonight,' he said, 'at the Tree

House Bar.' He looked at me. 'Do you want to come with me, Stella?'

I stopped smiling. 'Oh,' I replied, 'I can't. I'm sorry, Tony. I'm going to the cinema tonight.'

'That's OK,' Tony said, and he walked to his house.

I looked at Tony's back as he opened his front door. I didn't want to go to the cinema with Klaus now. I wanted to go out for a drink with Tony.

'How about tomorrow night?' I asked. Tony looked back at me and smiled.

'OK,' he said. 'Good. Eight o'clock then?'

I smiled at him. 'Eight o'clock tomorrow,' I replied.

I enjoyed going out with Klaus. The film was called *Dead Men Can't Speak*. It was a very bad film, but it made me and Klaus laugh.

'I need a drink after that,' Klaus said when we came out, and we went to a bar near the cinema.

'Sorry about the film, Stella,' he said when we had our drinks. 'Next time we can go to a film you want to see.'

But I just smiled and drank my drink. I liked Klaus, but I didn't want to think about next time now.

After the bar, Klaus walked home with me. I knew he wanted me to ask him into the house, but I didn't.

'Thank you for tonight, Klaus,' I said. 'I enjoyed it. See you tomorrow at work.'

I think he was a little sad, but he smiled anyway. 'OK, Stella,' he said. 'See you tomorrow.'

I opened my front door.

'Stella,' Klaus said behind me, and I looked at him.

'Yes?'

'I like you a lot.'

'Thank you,' I said. 'Good night.' Then I went into my house and closed the door. I didn't say, 'I like you too, Klaus,' because I didn't know what I thought. I liked him, but did I want to be his girlfriend or just his friend?

Chapter 4 *Drinks for two*

When I got home from work the next evening, I washed my hair and put on a new dress.

'You look nice,' Tony told me when we met at eight o'clock.

'Thank you,' I said. Tony's blue shirt was like the blue of his eyes. He looked good too.

'Bring your jacket. Then we can sit out,' he said. I got a jacket, and then we left.

'I love warm evenings,' Tony said as we walked down the street. 'When I first met Kathy, we lived in Scotland. It gets dark at eleven o'clock there at this time of year. I loved the long evenings.'

I didn't say anything, and he looked at me. 'Sorry,' he said. 'I know I talk about the old days a lot.'

'That's OK,' I said.

'No,' he said, 'it isn't OK. I don't want to think about the old days tonight. I just want to think about now.'

I was happy to hear that, and when I smiled at him, he smiled back.

'I want to know everything about you, Stella,' he told me.

'Everything?' I asked.

'Yes,' he said. 'Everything.'

There were lots of people in the garden at the Tree House Bar. Men and women sitting at small tables having conversations. Couples. And when Tony and I sat at a table, we were a couple, too.

'I like it here,' Tony said.

'Yes,' I said. 'I do too.'

Tony had his drink in his hand. He smiled at me. 'Here's to good neighbours,' he said.

'To good neighbours.'

Then Tony looked at me. 'Tell me about your job,' he said. 'What food do you like to cook?'

I thought about it. 'Food with lots of colour,' I said. 'I like my meals to look good. That's very important to me.'

'I must come and eat at your restaurant,' Tony said.

I spoke quickly, without thinking. 'Or I can cook for you at home,' I said.

Tony smiled.

'Yes please!' he said.

'I love my job,' I told him. 'When I was a child, I cooked with my mother.'

'Daisy likes to cook with her mother,' Tony told me. His face went sad. 'They make cakes. Kathy's a good cook too.'

I looked at him. 'What does Kathy do?' I asked.

'She's a teacher,' he told me. 'But I don't want to talk about Kathy. Tell me about you – your family. Where do they live?'

I told him and he listened, but I felt there were three people at the table now – me, Tony and Kathy.

I stopped talking about my family and looked at him. 'Tell me about you and Kathy,' I said.

Tony looked down at his drink. 'Kathy left me. She met Cameron at work,' he said. 'She left me because she wanted to be with him.'

'I loved someone, too,' I told him. 'James. But he had lots of girlfriends.'

Tony put his hand on mine. 'Do you want to meet someone new?' he asked.

'I don't know,' I said. 'I'm afraid.'

He smiled at me. 'Well, I'm also afraid,' he said. 'But I do like you, Stella. I like you a lot.'

'And I like you, Tony,' I said. As I looked at him, I knew how I felt about Klaus. Klaus and I were friends, that was all. I liked him and I laughed with him, but when Klaus looked at me, I didn't feel like this.

Tony looked into my eyes. 'Good,' he said. 'Then come to tea at the weekend. Daisy told me she wants to see you again, and I want to see you again, too.'

I went to tea with them on Sunday. We played football and got very hot. Then, when Daisy was in bed, Tony and I went into the garden. We sat and talked, and Tony took my hand in his. And then I looked up at him, and he kissed me . . .

The next day Klaus asked me to see a film with him again, but I told him I couldn't go. And when I met Janet for lunch, I told her about me and Tony. 'Everything's going very well.' I said. 'Tony makes me very happy.'

She looked at me. 'Does he talk about Kathy when he's with you?' she asked.

'He has to see Kathy because of Daisy,' I told her. 'But that's all.'

'Good,' Janet said. But she didn't smile.

I looked at her. 'It's OK, Janet,' I said. 'Tony's a good man. He wants to be with me.'

'Good,' said Janet again. 'Because I only want you to be happy, Stella.'

And I was happy – for two months. I saw Tony every day. Sometimes Daisy was with us, and sometimes it was just me and Tony. We went to see films, we walked in the park and I cooked meals for him. We talked and laughed a lot. Oh yes, I was very happy.

And then one evening in October everything changed. I left work to walk home and I saw James in a bar. He was with a woman. They were laughing, and they looked happy. 'He laughed with me like that when he was my boyfriend,' I thought, and I wanted to go into the restaurant to talk to the woman. I wanted to say to her, 'James is no good!' But I didn't. I just walked up the street. But I was sad for her.

Then, when I got back to Bridge Street, I saw Tony in front of his house. He was with a woman too – a woman I didn't know. I saw Tony look down into the woman's face. 'He looks at *me* like that,' I thought. 'He stands near *me* like that.'

The woman's hair was black and very long. She was beautiful. She said something and put her hand on Tony's arm. Then I saw Tony walk to his front door. He looked back at the woman and said something to her. I knew he wanted her to go into the house with him. 'Don't go in!' I thought. But she did go in. And Tony closed the door. I went into my house and closed my door.

I sat down and thought about James again. 'James always had lots of girlfriends. Does Tony want me *and* that woman?'

But I didn't know the answer.

Chapter 5   *Who is that woman?*

I didn't see Tony that evening, and he didn't phone me. When I left for work the next day, his car wasn't there. Was he with that woman?

'Are you OK?' Klaus asked me when I got to the restaurant.

'Yes, thank you,' I said. I didn't want to talk to him about Tony and the woman. I didn't want to talk to anyone about them. But I thought about them a lot . . . all day.

After work, I went quickly back to Bridge Street. But not to my house. I went to Tony's house.

'Hi,' he said when he came to the door. He looked tired, and he didn't kiss me. 'Come in.'

We went into the living room. He had a cup of coffee on the table.

'Sorry,' he said. 'Do you want something to drink?'

'No,' I said. 'I want to speak to you . . . about yesterday. I . . . I saw you with a woman.'

Tony looked down. 'Oh,' he said.

I waited for him to speak.

'It isn't what you think, Stella,' he said.

I looked at him.

'Stella, that was Kathy,' Tony said.

I sat down. I didn't know what to say.

'She wanted to talk to me.'

'About what?'

Tony didn't answer.

I thought about the two of them in the street. 'Tony,' I asked, 'do you still love Kathy?'

He looked up at me. 'No!' he said. 'Do you think that?'

'I don't know what to think.' I said.

Tony took my hand. 'Oh, Stella,' he said. 'Of course I don't still love Kathy.'

'You don't?' I asked. I looked into his eyes. James didn't like me to look into his eyes like that. But Tony looked back into my eyes. He didn't look away.

'Sometimes I want to hate Kathy,' he told me. 'But I can't. She's Daisy's mother.'

'I know you think about the time when you were a family,' I told him, 'you, Kathy and Daisy.'

'Yes,' he said, 'I do think about that. I think about it because of Daisy. But I don't want to be with Kathy now, Stella. I want to be with you.'

Now I couldn't look at him. I felt small and afraid. 'Do you?' I asked.

'Yes,' he said. 'You know I do. I like you, Stella. I like you a lot. Actually . . .'

I looked up at him again. 'Yes?'

He smiled at me. 'Actually, I think I love you, Stella. No, I *know* I love you.'

I was happy again. 'Oh, Tony,' I said, 'I love you too!'

'Come here,' he said, and he kissed me. But I knew there was still something wrong.

'Kathy came here yesterday because she wanted to tell me something,' he said. 'She and Cameron want to live in Scotland. They want to buy a house there, and they . . . they want to take Daisy with them.'

I looked at him. 'Oh, Tony,' I said. 'She can't do that!'

24

Tony looked down again. 'I think she can,' he said. 'She's Daisy's mother, and Daisy lives with her. Cameron has a new job in Scotland, and Kathy can get a job there as a teacher.'

'But Daisy needs you too!' I said.

Tony couldn't answer for a minute. He was too sad. Then he tried to smile. 'I don't know what to do, Stella,' he said. 'I just don't know what to do.'

'We can speak to someone who can help us. A lawyer,' I said. 'We can stop her! That's what we can do!'

Tony looked at me. 'We can try,' he said.

Chapter 6 *A family again*

So we went to see a lawyer – a Mrs Scott.

'I can talk to Kathy's lawyer,' she told us, 'and then, we can go to the Family Court.' She looked at Tony. 'But I must tell you, Mr Bryant, it isn't going to be easy. The Family Courts often think a child needs to be with his or her mother.'

'Daisy needs her father too!' I said, and Mrs Scott smiled.

'Yes,' she said. 'I know that. We can only try.'

'Thank you,' said Tony. Then we left.

The next two days were not easy. Then Mrs Scott phoned and said that the Family Court was next Tuesday.

Daisy came to us the weekend before the Family Court. The weather was bad, so we watched TV.

There was a film about horses on television. Daisy looked up at us. 'Cameron says I can have a horse when we live in Scotland,' she said. 'He wants to teach me all about horses.'

'That's nice,' Tony said. But I knew he was sad. I took his hand.

'But I want *you* to teach me about horses, Daddy,' Daisy said.

When he heard that, Tony smiled.

'Can you teach me, Daddy?' Daisy asked. Tony gave her a kiss.

'Yes, baby,' he said.

But that evening when Daisy was in bed, Tony looked at me. 'What do I know about horses?' he said. 'Nothing. I only know about computers.'

'No you don't,' I said. 'You know how to love Daisy and that's what's important.'

He kissed me and smiled. 'I'm very happy I came to live next door to you, Stella Greenwood,' he said.

On Tuesday, we went to the Family Court. Kathy was there with her lawyer and Cameron. Daisy was at home with Kathy's mother.

Tony's hand was in mine. He didn't look over at Kathy or Cameron.

Then the judge came into the court. He was a small man with grey hair.

28

We were in the Court for thirty minutes. Mrs Scott spoke for Tony and Kathy's lawyer spoke for Kathy. The judge listened and he asked some questions. Mrs Scott and Kathy's lawyer answered them.

Then the judge looked at us and . . . and he said what we didn't want him to say.

'I'm sorry, Mr Bryant . . .'

I think that's all I heard him say. I just sat next to Tony and thought, 'No! No, no, no!'

Tony put his head in his hands. He didn't say anything, but I knew he was angry.

When the judge and the lawyers left the court, Kathy came over to talk to Tony. But he didn't want to look at her.

'You can still see Daisy at any time, Tony,' she told him, but he didn't answer. Then Kathy left with Cameron.

I sat there next to Tony. I didn't know what to say to him. But then I thought about what Janet always said to me. 'When you want to do something, just do it. Don't stop and think! Don't wait! Just do it.' And I knew what I wanted to do. 'Tony,' I said, 'Look at me.'

His face was white. I took his hands and looked into his eyes. 'Look,' I said. 'There are computers in Scotland. And lots of restaurants.'

'What are you saying?' he asked.

I smiled. 'I'm saying we can live near Daisy. I'm saying . . . we can go to Scotland.'

Tony smiled at me. A big smile. 'Me and you?' he said.

'Yes,' I said. 'Me . . . you . . . and Daisy too.'

And, in January, that's what we did. We went to live in Scotland. I got a job as a chef at a hotel, and Tony got a good job with computers.

And Daisy? Well, we see her every weekend. She's teaching Tony about horses.

Cambridge English Readers

Look out for other titles in this series:

Level 1

Parallel
Colin Campbell

'Max sat on his bed. There was a gun on the bed beside him. The gun was still warm.'
Max kills people for money. But one day he goes to a new world and his life changes.

Help!
Philip Prowse

Frank Wormold is a writer. To help him finish one of his stories he starts to use a computer. But the computer gives him more help than he wants. Then he really needs 'help'!

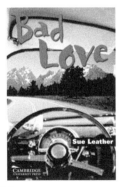

Bad Love
Sue Leather

'Dr. Jack Daly?' Judy said. 'He's famous.'
'I don't often like famous people,' I said.
'Oh, come on, Detective Laine!'
One week later Daly is dead and Flick Laine is looking for his killer.

Just Like a Movie
Sue Leather

Brad Black and his girlfriend Gina like the movies. They are happy, but they have no money. Then Brad has an idea and thinks that real life can be just like the movies – and that's when things go wrong.

Level 2

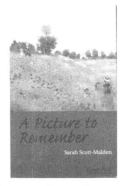

Different Worlds
Margaret Johnson

'In my world there are no birds singing. There are no noisy men working on the roads. No babies crying.'

Sam is like any other teenage girl except that she was born deaf. Now she is in love with Jim, but are their worlds too different?

A Picture to Remember
Sarah Scott-Malden

Christina Rinaldo works for the Museo Nacional de Bellas Artes in Buenos Aires. One day she has a motorbike accident and can't remember some things. But there are two men who think she remembers too much, and they want to kill her before she tells the police what she saw.

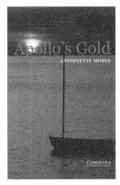

Jojo's Story
Antoinette Moses

'There aren't any more days. There's just time. Time when it's dark and time when it's light. Everything is dead, so why not days too?'

Everyone in Jojo's village is dead, and ten-year-old Jojo is alone.

Apollo's Gold
Antoinette Moses

Liz studies and teaches archaeology in Athens. She goes on holiday to the beautiful and peaceful island of Sifnos. But the peace does not last long when one of the local men dies, and Liz becomes involved with some very dangerous people.

32